S0-ABB-500

I Spy
coloring book
for Kids

This Book belongs to:

I SPY WITH MY LITTLE EYE
SOMETHING STARTING WITH

It's an Apple

I SPY WITH MY LITTLE EYE
SOMETHING STARTING WITH

It's a
Bat

I SPY WITH MY LITTLE EYE SOMETHING STARTING WITH

It's a Cat

I SPY WITH MY LITTLE EYE
SOMETHING STARTING WITH

It's a Dress

I SPY WITH MY LITTLE EYE
SOMETHING STARTING WITH

It's Eyes

I SPY WITH MY LITTLE EYE
SOMETHING STARTING WITH

It's

Frankenstein

I SPY WITH MY LITTLE EYE
SOMETHING STARTING WITH

It's a Ghost

I SPY WITH MY LITTLE EYE
SOMETHING STARTING WITH

H

It's a

House

I SPY WITH MY LITTLE EYE
SOMETHING STARTING WITH

It's an
Ice cream

I SPY WITH MY LITTLE EYE
SOMETHING STARTING WITH

It's a
Jack-O-Lantern

I SPY WITH MY LITTLE EYE
SOMETHING STARTING WITH

It's a Kite

I SPY WITH MY LITTLE EYE
SOMETHING STARTING WITH

It's a Leaf

I SPY WITH MY LITTLE EYE
SOMETHING STARTING WITH

It's a Mummy

I SPY WITH MY LITTLE EYE
SOMETHING STARTING WITH

It's a Neck

I SPY WITH MY LITTLE EYE SOMETHING STARTING WITH

It's an Owl

I SPY WITH MY LITTLE EYE SOMETHING STARTING WITH

It's a Pumpkin

I SPY WITH MY LITTLE EYE
SOMETHING STARTING WITH

It's a
Queen

I SPY WITH MY LITTLE EYE
SOMETHING STARTING WITH

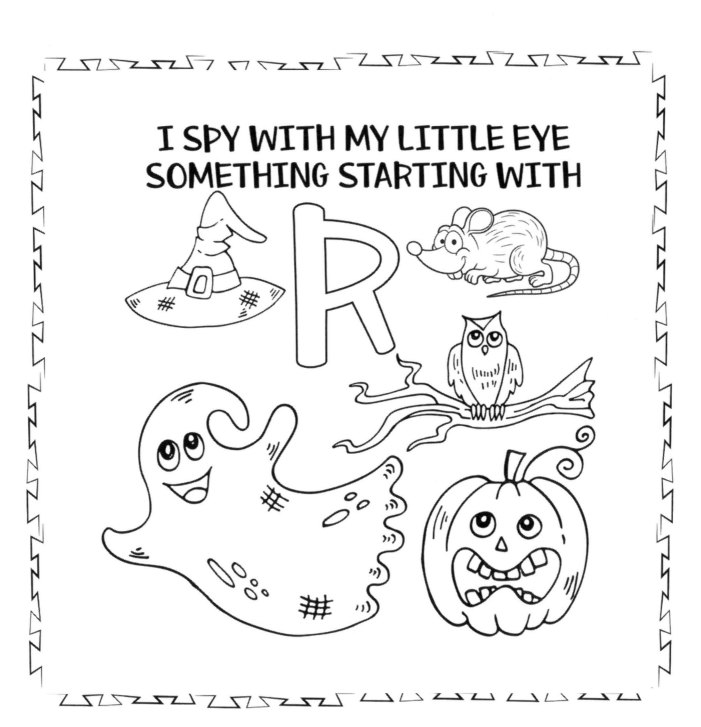

It's a Rat

I SPY WITH MY LITTLE EYE
SOMETHING STARTING WITH

It's a
Spider

I SPY WITH MY LITTLE EYE
SOMETHING STARTING WITH

It's a Tree

I SPY WITH MY LITTLE EYE
SOMETHING STARTING WITH

It's an Umbrella

I SPY WITH MY LITTLE EYE SOMETHING STARTING WITH

It's a Vampire

I SPY WITH MY LITTLE EYE SOMETHING STARTING WITH

It's a Witch

I SPY WITH MY LITTLE EYE
SOMETHING STARTING WITH

It's an X-ray costume

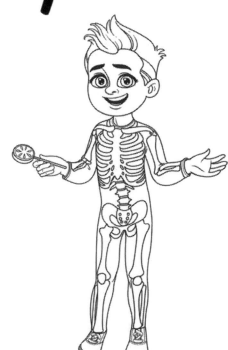

I SPY WITH MY LITTLE EYE
SOMETHING STARTING WITH

It's a Yo-yo

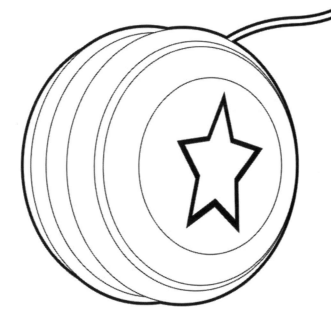

I SPY WITH MY LITTLE EYE SOMETHING STARTING WITH

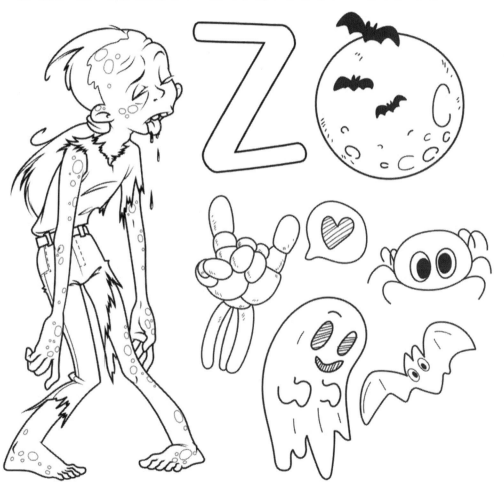

It's a
Zombie

Made in the USA
Middletown, DE
08 September 2021

47847998R00060